THE GHOSTLY TALES OF LOUISIANA

Published by Arcadia Children's Books
A Division of Arcadia Publishing, Inc.
Charleston, SC
www.arcadiapublishing.com

Copyright © 2025 by Arcadia Children's Books
All rights reserved

Spooky America is a trademark of Arcadia Publishing, Inc.

First published 2025
Manufactured in the United States

Designed by Jessica Nevins
Images used courtesy of Shutterstock.com; p. 86 William A. Morgan/Shutterstock.com; p. 94 Suzanne C. Grim/Shutterstock.com.

ISBN: 9781467197878
Library of Congress Control Number: 2024950548

Notice: The information in this book is true and complete to the best of our knowledge. It is offered without guarantee on the part of the author or Arcadia Publishing. The author and Arcadia Publishing disclaim all liability in connection with the use of this book.

All rights reserved. No part of this book may be reproduced or transmitted in any form whatsoever without prior written permission from the publisher except in the case of brief quotations embodied in critical articles and reviews.

Spooky America
THE GHOSTLY TALES OF LOUISIANA

LISHA CAUTHEN

Adapted from Haunted Louisiana by Barbara Sillery

Table of Contents & Map Key

Welcome to Spooky Louisiana! 3

1. Chapter 1. An Island of Ghosts and More 9
2. Chapter 2. Pirates and Skullduggery 19
3. Chapter 3. Bottles and Spirits 33
4. Chapter 4. Chilling Apparitions, Hair-raising Noises, and Proof . 43
5. Chapter 5. A House Full of Ghosts 55
6. Chapter 6. The Keeper of the Castle 65
7. Chapter 7. All Ghosts Are Not the Same 77
8. Chapter 8. Love Gone Wrong 87
9. Chapter 9. Restless in the City of the Dead 95

A Ghostly Goodbye 107

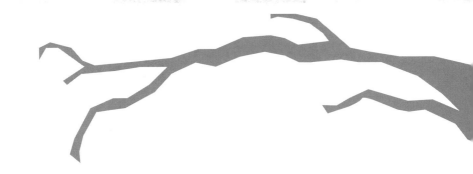

Welcome to Spooky Louisiana!

Imagine it's January 1814, and you have answered General Andrew Jackson's call to defend New Orleans, Louisiana, and the United States of America. You and your father have joined 4,000 other men and boys (and perhaps women in male disguise) who are soldiers, farmers, businessmen, aristocrats, freedmen, enslaved people, Native Americans, and pirates to fight the British.

The British have amassed their ships near the mouth of the Mississippi River and are now coming ashore for the attack. You grip your rifle, your mouth dry but your resolve strong, as you crouch behind a miles-long barricade of logs, dirt, and mud-covered cotton bales known as Line Jackson.

Louisiana has long been worth fighting for. In 1682, Robert de La Salle sailed all the way down the Mississippi River to the Gulf of Mexico, where he planted a cross and claimed the entire Mississippi River basin for France. He named the territory Louisiana, after King Louis XIV. His claim stretched from the Great Lakes to the Gulf of Mexico and from the Allegheny Mountains in the east to the Rocky Mountains in the west.

Through the 1700s, French, Spanish, and German settlers moved in, establishing farms that grew into plantations, and building bustling ports on the Mississippi River and the Gulf of Mexico. The French governed Louisiana until 1803, when Napoleon Bonaparte needed money to fight his wars in Europe. Napoleon sold 828,000 square miles of territory of this North American claim to the United States for fifteen million. This deal is called the Louisiana Purchase, and it is how the United States acquired land that became all or part of fifteen modern states located between the Mississippi River and the Rocky Mountains. Louisiana was admitted to the Union in 1812 as a full-fledged state.

Now, you and your neighbors are U.S. citizens, and you are fighting for your country.

You cower as the first volley of British artillery screams overhead. You can feel each explosion rumble in the pit of your stomach, and your ears ring. Soon, the U.S. artillery answers. Both sides bombard each other, but Jean Lafitte and his band of pirates have brought a deadly amount of canons, rifles, and ammunition to the fight in exchange for a pardon of their pirating crimes.

The U.S. forces outlast the British in this first round of the battle. You swallow, hard, because you know more is coming, and you are ready to defend your home.

The moment comes when 8,000 British troops assault Line Jackson. Many fall before they get to you, but a few break through, climbing over logs and scrambling over cotton bales, their bayonets gleaming in the sun.

In the end, you and your father escape with minor injuries from the brief but bloody Battle of New Orleans, which ends in victory for the new state of Louisiana. It is the last battle of the War of 1812; this success assures the United States is respected throughout the world.

And the people of Louisiana are a big part of that.

The fight for freedom never ends, and in the coming years, slavery will divide the country. Many Americans will insist that slavery must be abolished, but the Southern economy will depend on the labor of enslaved Black men and women. In 1861, Louisiana will secede from the Union and fight on the side of the Confederate States of America during the Civil War. After much suffering, the war will end in a Union victory, the enslaved people will be freed, and the Black community will continue its struggle for equality

Now, come back to the present, where you will discover a state that is vibrant, exciting, and modern. However, you will also find that many who built Louisiana—rich, poor, free, and enslaved—still haunt the byways of this beautiful state. So, if you dare, go on a ghost hunt through the bayous, plantation homes, restaurant kitchens, and cemeteries of Louisiana. Because the phantoms and specters you will meet are dying to tell their stories...

CHAPTER 1

An Island of Ghosts and More

Where better to start your quest for ghosts, monsters, and other supernatural beings than a place known as *Île Phantom*, which is French for "Ghost Island"?

Île Phantom is located just outside New Orleans in the marshes of Bayou Segnette, a name that means "Blessed Bayou." But *Île Phantom* is anything but blessed.

A bayou is a broad wetland home to a

diverse variety of wildlife such as the American alligator, great blue heron, armadillos, crawfish, otters, bobcats, and even bald eagles. You will find all these incredible animals as you travel along Bayou Segnette, but once you arrive on *Île Phantom*, you may encounter some... *otherworldly* creatures.

Ask someone with a flatboat to take you across the still, brackish water to *Île Phantom*. There you will find tangled Spanish moss hanging from ancient trees where screech owls roost. Cypress trees with thick, twisted roots that wade in the murky waters like a crew of giants. Venomous water moccasins that slither in fan-like palmetto thickets along the shore.

But if luck is not on your side, you may also meet the island monsters that have haunted the families who have lived in the area for generations.

The Native Americans were the first to encounter the eerie creatures on *Île Phantom*, and they warned the Acadians who arrived in 1785 to avoid the island. The Acadians were French pioneers who first settled in Canada, but after a series of wars with the British, they were expelled from their new home. Though some Acadians managed to stay in Canada, a large group resettled in Louisiana, bringing their language and culture with them. Today, they are known as Cajuns.

When the Acadians met the Native Americans already living here, they quickly learned to avoid *Île Phantom* because the *coquin l'eau*, *loup-garou*, and *feu follet* that live here are less than welcoming.

When your boat bumps against the shore and

you wade onto the island, the first unnatural creature you may encounter is the *coquin l'eau*, which means "water devil." Stay calm, because the *coquin l'eau* is more of a nuisance than a terrifying demon. It is said to live in the swamp water, waiting for a chance to pull a sneaky prank on you. Most often, he waits until you are pleasantly relaxed or full from a good meal and decide to take an evening stroll. You will never see him coming because the *coquin l'eau* is patient. He will wait until just the right moment to trip you when you least expect it. You may stumble, you may fall, but his mischievousness is seldom life-threatening; it's simply annoying.

A more hazardous otherworldly creature on *Île Phantom* is the *feu follet*, which is the French name for the "will-o'-the-wisp." The name will-o'-the-wisp sounds delicate and beautiful, but that is deceiving. Most traditional tales of will-o'-the-wisps describe them as fairies or spirits. But the *feu follet* is a much more strange and disturbing spirit. It is the ghost of a baby who died before weaning, which means before it could eat solid food, and it appears as unsettling lights in swamps or woods. New parents in Louisiana are warned to watch for the *feu follet* because it may find its way into their baby's nursery. If their child wakes up with rosy cheeks, the parents know that the *feu follet* has been sucking away the baby's breath.

To protect their child from the *feu follet*, parents scatter mustard seeds underneath their baby's crib. Why mustard seeds? Because the *feu follet* is compelled to stop what it is doing and count the mustard seeds, which are as tiny as a speck of black pepper. Even if the monstrous ghost-baby gets close to a final tally, it will lose count of the seeds and have to start all over again.

One family experienced a terrifying visit

from the *feu follet*. The family lived on land that had once been a plantation, with gigantic oak trees nearly 300 years old. One night, the father was away and the mother was home with the children, all by herself.

Trying to unwind after a long day, the mother glanced out the window and saw an odd, yellow light shining through the trees. The family never

had visitors, and it was too soon for her husband to be home. That could mean only one thing—the *feu follet*. The mother did not know about spreading mustard seeds to confuse the *feu follet*, but she did have a plan.

Quickly, she blew out all the lamps in the house. She hid the children underneath their beds, putting her finger to her lips to warn them to stay still and quiet. And then she sat in her rocker, watching out the window, guarding against the ghostly visitor and waiting for sun up.

Later, when the children asked about the *feu follet* and why she had hidden them underneath their beds, their mother said she had been teasing and the light they'd seen through the trees was just the moon. But if that were true, why did she leave the children under the bed and the lamps blown out all night until the sun was up and their father was home?

Some say the *feu follet* is just swamp gas, but if you see a strange light coming toward you through the trees on *Île Phantom*, are you going to take a chance?

Of all the inhuman inhabitants on *Île Phantom*, perhaps the most terrifying is the *loup-garou*, which is the French name for "werewolf." However, in Louisiana, the term *loup-garou* has morphed into the name "*rougarou*," which describes a much more frightening monster. The *rougarou* can assume more forms than a human or a wolf; it is a shapeshifter that can take on any form it wishes. Parents warn their children that even a flower might, in fact, be a *rougarou*. And if you pick it, the *rougarou* may suddenly grow fangs, bite you on the neck, and enchant you so that you spend the rest of your life dancing among the wolves.

The *rougarou* prefers bayous, swamps, and uninhabited places just like *Île Phantom*. He can fly, slither, run on four legs, or rise up on two. When you visit the island, if you see a shadow scampering out of the corner of your eye, don't assume it's simply a harmless dog, possum, or raccoon.

And whatever you do, don't pick any flowers.

Île Phantom is crowded with a variety of supernatural beings, but it got its name because of pirates, murder, and treasure. And if you want to know the story, turn the page...

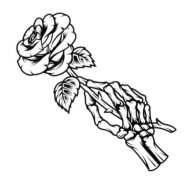

Bayou Barataria

CHAPTER 2

Pirates and Skullduggery

Though *Île Phantom* is a forbidding place, one area of the island is even spookier than the rest. It is where dying cypress trees with ghostly white trunks rise in the moonlight. Here, it is said that the scoundrel pirate Jean Lafitte buried his treasure—and more.

Though Jean Lafitte had a French name and spoke with a French accent, no one is sure exactly when and where he was born. But by the beginning of the 1800s, Jean Lafitte was the scourge of ships sailing in the Gulf of Mexico. With his brother, Pierre, he ran a vast black-market business selling the booty they stole. Jean Lafitte was at times a pirate, privateer, militia member, and spy.

There is a difference between a pirate and a privateer. A pirate is an outlaw who attacks any ship he chooses and keeps the loot for himself. A privateer is an outlaw granted a letter of marque, which is a license to attack the enemies of the country that issued the letter. The privateer keeps a portion of the loot and turns the rest over to the country that sponsors him.

No one knows exactly when Jean Lafitte

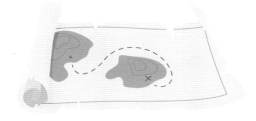

buried his treasure on *Île Phantom*, nor do they know whether Lafitte was acting as a pirate or a privateer. We do know that the wide channel leading to the island was on the main waterway between the pirate's hidden warehouses in Barataria and New Orleans, where he sold his ill-gotten goods. We know that Jean Lafitte buried treasure all along the Louisiana and Texas gulf coasts. And we are told that where he buried treasure, he also buried one of his men to serve as a ghostly guard.

Many have searched *Île Phantom* for Lafitte's treasure, and none have been successful because the old pirate's faithful guard still protects his master's booty. If you are brave enough to pick up your shovel and try your luck, beware—many report being chased by a ghost that is dripping seaweed, dressed in pirate clothes like blue breeches and a striped shirt, and carrying a cutlass, or curved sword, tucked inside a red sash around his waist. Watch out—that cutlass may be hundreds of years old, but it is still sharp!

If you want to meet Jean Lafitte himself, travel to Destrehan Manor, a plantation home on the Mississippi River, just outside of New Orleans. Built by a hired freedman of mixed ancestry in 1790, it is the oldest plantation home in the lower Mississippi Valley. The home has been rescued and restored after the old pirate almost destroyed it—from the grave.

The first eerie reports surfaced sometime in the 1800s and continue to this day. Witnesses claim that on foggy nights, a figure can be seen dressed in dated clothing, a wide-brimmed hat on his head, pointing at the plantation home. Who could it be?

Many have concluded that the specter is Jean Lafitte himself. It has been whispered that one of the Destrehans was an acquaintance of Lafitte and may have allowed him to hide some treasure on his property—and that the pirate booty is still there. That rumor sparked the near-destruction of Destrehan Manor.

For decades, treasure hunters vandalized the home, frantically searching for pirate gold. They broke through walls and exposed the original bousillage, or mud and moss insulation. They dug holes in ceilings and floors. They smashed marble mantels. The structure of the house was close to collapse.

Finally, in the 1960s, the River Road Historical Society stepped in and saved the home, which you can tour today. But if you do, don't pay any attention to the ghostly Lafitte, pointing through the mist, because no one has ever found any treasure.

Does that mean there isn't any? Or . . . is the treasure still waiting to be found?

Lafitte served in the American militia during the Battle of New Orleans. A few years later, he and his pirate crew left Barataria for Galveston, Texas, where they continued their pirating ways. Lafitte also spied for the Spanish during the Mexican War for Independence. In the 1820s, Jean Lafitte disappeared from the pages of history. Some say he was killed while attempting to pirate a ship. Others believe he faked his own death and went into hiding, dying in old age.

Though Lafitte was gone, he left behind a ragtag crew of pirates with no leader. By the late 1830s, the men were in disarray and desperate for money. Seven of these pirates decided to visit an old acquaintance in Louisiana at Chretien Point Plantation. And one of them never left.

Hypolite Chretien built Chretien Point Plantation.

He was an old friend of Lafitte's. They are said to have met on the battlefield at New Orleans, when Hypolite saved a wounded Lafitte. After the war, the two turned their friendship into a thriving business.

Hypolite and his wife, Felicité, grew cotton, but Jean Lafitte had a proposition that would make them rich beyond their dreams. The old pirate had moved his operations to Galveston, and he needed a place to sell his stolen merchandise back in Louisiana. Hypolite and Felicité had such a place—Chretien Point. They hosted "garden parties" for the richest people in the area. But the garden parties were really giant garage sales where the pirates could peddle their stolen goods. Under the boughs of the oak, pecan, and tallow trees, men in top hats, waistcoats, and gleaming boots bargained with harder, battle-tested men who wore tattered clothes and had weather-lined faces.

The Chretiens made so much money, they built an impressive home in 1831. Hypolite didn't trust banks, so he buried caches of gold around his property. Unfortunately, soon after their mansion was built, Hypolite died of yellow fever and left Felicité to manage their businesses. By then, Lafitte had disappeared from the scene, and seven of his former pirates remembered the stories of gold buried around Chretien Point Plantation and decided the lonely, rich widow, Felicité, would be easy to rob.

They were very wrong.

Felicité was a liberated woman for her time. She rode her horse astride, like a man, rather than sidesaddle, like ladies did. She won large amounts of cash playing poker. Her father didn't pay her husband-to-be a dowry (money or goods that fathers traditionally gave to the man their daughter would marry); in fact, Hypolite paid Felicité for the pleasure of her hand in marriage! She was smart, daring, and brave.

So, when Felicité heard a strange horse neighing outside one night as she was putting her children to bed, she did not panic.

She peeked out the window and saw seven dark figures coming toward her home. Quickly, she went to her chest of drawers and pulled out a handful of jewelry and a pistol. Then she stood on the landing at the top of the stairs and waited in the gloom lit only by one, flickering candle.

The boldest pirate slowly creaked open the front door and peered into the house. Felicité rattled the jewelry in her hand, teasing the pirate, while she hid the gun behind her. Greed flickered in the pirate's eyes as he clomped across the floor in his muddy boots and started up the stairs toward Felicité . . .

Blam!

The pirate fell dead on the eleventh step.

Felicité and her servants chased away the rest of the pirates. But the pirate that Felicité shot remains in the plantation home. People who live in the home today call the pirate ghost "Robert," and Robert still holds a grudge.

One night, the present owner of the plantation home invited a bus tour to visit. The owner told the tourists the story of how Robert had died. He laughed at how Felicité tricked the pirate into coming close enough to shoot dead.

Robert must have been listening to the owner ridiculing him. Because at 5:00 a.m. the next morning, while the owner was asleep, his

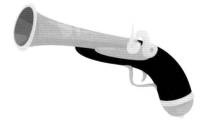

car horn suddenly began to blare for no reason. The owner awoke with a start, threw on his slippers, and ran outside to his car. Instead of disconnecting the wires, he reached inside the window and "pushed" an invisible hand away from the steering wheel.

The car horn stopped.

The owner went back to bed, but an hour later, the car horn started up again. He knew just what to do. He ran outside and pushed the invisible hand away from the steering wheel, and again, the honking topped. Was it Robert, angry because the owner had laughed at how he had died?

A few days later, the owner was telling the story about the car horn to some dinner guests. One of the guests argued with him, insisting that there was a rational explanation because there was no such things as ghosts. The guest pounded on the table with both hands, shouting, "Ghosts can't make things happen!"

All the guests jumped because the double front doors in the dining room flew open—but *how*? They had been latched tight.

The owner refused to be intimidated. Months later, he was leading an evening tour through the historic plantation rooms, which are filled with antiques. Ever the entertainer, the owner couldn't resist telling the story, once again, of how the foolish pirate fell for Felicité's deception and was shot to death on the stairs.

What do you think happened?

Yes. Once again, at 5:00 a.m., his car horn began screaming. For the second time, he staggered down the stairs and out the door to push away the invisible hand on the steering wheel.

Today, the owner has finally learned his

lesson. Once a skeptic, he no longer makes fun of Robert.

When you visit Chretien Point Plantation, show Robert a little respect, and he will show you the same. But if curiosity gets the best of you, take a look at the eleventh step on the staircase, where you can still see the bloodstain from the pirate whose greed killed him.

CHAPTER 3

Bottles and Spirits

If you visit Magnolia Lane Plantation in Westwego, you will walk under trees dripping with Spanish moss.

And bottles.

They sway and clank eerily in the warm breeze—tall bottles, squat bottles, bottles with and without handles. They hang from long wires attached to scraggly tree limbs, their mouths open to the rainwater that collects inside them.

These bottles are hung in the trees to ward off evil spirits; it's an Afro-Caribbean Voodoo tradition that enslaved people brought with them to Louisiana.

Magnolia Lane Plantation was built in 1784, but Richard Naberschnig's family has owned the home since 1867. Naberschnig is the one who hung the spirit bottles back in the 1970s, when the home was overcome by violent noises and strange apparitions.

One room, in particular, was a problem—the front bedroom. Because of the unnerving noises and shadowy figures she often saw, Naberschnig's mother declared the front bedroom a bad room and always kept the door firmly closed and locked. A well-educated woman, she was nonetheless afraid of the room because so many people had died there.

Which is why it came to be called the Dying Room.

Great-great-grandparents, great-grandparents, and grandparents all met their fate in the Dying Room. After the last death, Naberschnig's mother ordered the cursed room to be locked and never used again.

But Naberschnig didn't listen. When he moved back to the family home as an adult in 1976, he unlocked the Dying Room. The bed, where so many had taken their last breath, had not been slept in for fifty years. Determined to prove all the stories and fears were just superstitions, Naberschnig moved into the room.

He was in for a surprise.

The very first night, he heard gut-churning, heavy breathing. It came from the corner of the room—*huuhh, huuhh, huuhh*.

Naberschnig's hair stood on end—who was in the room? Was it his grandfather, great-grandfather, or even great-*great*-grandfather, gasping to take one more breath?

He was frightened—we can all understand that. But it's hard to understand why he decided to sleep in the Dying Room a second night. When again he heard the labored, torturous breathing, he said, "Whoever you are, I'm staying here. You can keep doing whatever you're doing." From then on, he coexisted with the ghosts who live in Magnolia Lane Plantation.

Naberschnig's mother is gone now, but he claims to still sense her presence in the home. Often, when walking around the house at night, goosebumps rise on his arms, and he knows she's near.

But his mother is not the only one still roaming the house.

He claims that the furnishings in the house have not changed since 1867, which may account for the company of so many ghosts.

One of those ghosts is the spirit that haunts the attic. Naberschnig has seen the attic ghost many times, though he is not sure who it is. Is it a spirit from the distant past, when the home was first built? Or is it a ghostly member of Naberschnig's own family? If you dare to climb the creaky, steep, narrow staircase, there's a good chance you will catch a glimpse of the gloomy, spectral resident. Will it be enough to convince you that there really is a spiritual world and that ghosts exist?

Take a walk around the grounds and you will find that Magnolia Lane Plantation has its own hanging tree, though no one is sure whose lives were cut short at the end of a rope there, or why. Across the South, many innocent Black persons were accused of crimes they didn't commit. If you find a hanging tree far from a courthouse or jail, you can be sure that victims were executed without a legal trial. Perhaps the restless spirit of an innocent man haunts the grounds, because beyond the hanging tree, you will find a graveyard where shadows and shapes have been seen looming among the headstones.

After spending many nights in the Dying Room, meeting the attic spirit, and watching spooks dance around the graveyard, does Naberschnig believe in ghosts? "This house is haunted," he says, "because any place that doesn't change like this and hasn't for two hundred years, there are likely to be some people still here..."

Travel farther south along the Mississippi River and you will find Woodland Plantation, which is also known as "The Plantation on a Bottle." Once, 360 plantations lined both banks of this stretch of the Mississippi. Now, all the plantations are gone except one.

Woodland Plantation was built by one of the

country's first chief river pilots. It has withstood floods, hurricanes, yellow fever, and war. The home was used as a headquarters by the Union Army during the Civil War, and therefore, was left intact. After the Civil War, the plantation prospered, and later, the home was memorialized on the label of Southern Comfort whiskey, the "Grand Old Drink of the South."

But the plantation's fortunes turned, and by the 1920s, it was abandoned. The building fell into disrepair as squatters moved in and vandals took whatever they wanted. Finally, Woodland Plantation went to auction in 1997, when the Creppel family stepped in to buy it, and the long years of renovation began.

Which seems to have awakened the long-dormant ghosts.

As work began, Foster Creppel

lived in the derelict home, along with owls in the attic and alligators in the drainage pit.

He also shared his home with a lead-footed presence.

For the first few months, phantom footsteps pounded incessantly across the second floor above his head. Foster didn't know who the ghost was—the loud thumping seemed to be too heavy to be a woman or child. Was it the river pilot? Could it be an enslaved house servant going about his daily chores? Whoever it was, the spirit wanted to stay anonymous, because he lurked in the shadows and never showed his face. When Foster first camped out in the dilapidated building, the ghost woke him every night, pounding across the second floor. No matter how many times Foster raced up the stairs to catch the intruder, he always found himself alone.

The Creppels worked hard on restoring Woodland Plantation to its former glory. It took years to shovel out all the dirt, debris, and rotten timbers in the sadly neglected home. Little by little, the Creppels cleaned, polished, painted, and wallpapered the building. When you visit, don't expect to meet the lead-footed ghost stomping his way across the second floor, because Foster claims that once the work on the home was completed, the inconsiderate specter seemed to have settled down.

However, the Creppels continue to sponsor archeological investigations on the property and plan to resurrect the overseer's cabin and the old sugar mill.

What ghosts will they stir up this time?

Oak Alley Plantation

Chilling Apparitions, Hair-raising Noises, and Proof

Oak Alley Plantation in Vacherie—about fifty miles west of New Orleans—is famous for the twenty-eight live oak trees lining the road that stretches for a quarter mile between the Mississippi River and the front door of the grand home. As you walk under the leafy, green tunnel, known as Oak Alley, thank the unknown French settler who planted the saplings in the early 1700s—more than 300 years ago.

Oak Alley was here long before the Oak Alley Plantation home, which was built in the 1830s by Jacques Roman for his bride, Celina. Celina was proud of the impressive home—so proud, she has never left.

Proof? Ask the tourists who snapped some photos in the main bedroom of Oak Alley Plantation. In the photo, the sun streams in to reveal a wooden breakfast tray resting on the four-poster bed. A doll dressed in period clothing lays in an intricately carved, rosewood cradle. A bowl of flowers sits on the chest of drawers, placed underneath an oval mirror hanging on the wall. It is a moment from a typical morning in 1837.

The tourists were so taken with the scene, they snapped photo after photo. To their surprise, one photo was not like the others. Because in this photo, they captured a tiny young woman standing at the French windows, looking out upon the lush plantation grounds. Dressed in a hoop-skirt dress with long sleeves and a high collar, the figure is topped by a stream of dark curls spilling down her back. Even more surprising, the figure can be seen reflected in the mirror.

But minus a head.

The tourists who took the eerie photograph asked the staff at the plantation for an explanation—but the staff members had none. They could only conclude that the "Lady of Illusion" was Celina Roman herself, the first mistress of Oak Alley Plantation, still admiring her beautiful estate.

Celina is not the only mistress of this

plantation who couldn't bear to see her happy days here come to an end. Another woman has materialized to scold the staff for not taking care of her home well enough.

It seems that one night, a terrible storm soaked the area. The security alarm notified the director of a problem at the plantation home, so he drove over to check things out. He rushed inside the building and into the children's nursery upstairs, and he found the door blown open and rain pouring inside.

The director shut the doors firmly and started downstairs to get a mop to clean up the mess. But when he got to the third-to-last step, he felt a violent push from behind. Caught off guard, the director fell the rest of the way down the stairs and ended up on his knees. After he caught his breath, he turned around to see who had assaulted him, but no one was there.

That is... no one he could see.

"Don't do that to me again!" he warned. And so far, the ghost has not.

Who was the vicious spirit who pushed the director down the stairs? Many staff members report seeing the apparition of a woman sitting on the end of the bed occupied by the last private owner of the estate, Josephine. But why attack the director? Is she upset that the caretakers allowed her precious children's nursery to get drenched with rain? Or is she simply annoyed by all the strangers taking tours through her beloved home?

If you'd like to meet a younger, less violent ghost, visit the "Little Girl Lost" who haunts the Lafitte Guest House on the corner of Bourbon and St. Phillip streets in the French Quarter district in New Orleans. A humble home built and occasionally occupied by the Lafitte brothers once stood on this corner, but the current building was built in 1849 as a home for a businessman and his family.

Many visitors report seeing a tiny, confused little girl who exits Room 22, meanders down the hall, and stumbles into a gilt-framed, five-foot mirror at one end of the second-floor landing. Other visitors, unaware of the sad ghost child and weary after a day of travel, have climbed the stairs to relax in their hotel room, only to see the reflection of the crying little girl in the mirror on the landing. The phantom is so real, they whirl around to comfort the sobbing child.

But as you might have guessed, no one is there.

Researchers believe that Room 22 was once the family nursery, and that the child's name is Marie. But which Marie?

CHILLING APPARITIONS, HAIR-RAISING NOISES, AND PROOF

Five little girls named Marie have lived in the building that has become the Lafitte Guest House. All five little girls died before their fifth birthday. Many diseases killed children before antibiotics were invented—cholera, tuberculosis, and pneumonia, to name a few. But in Louisiana, yellow fever was often the cause. The City of New Orleans has endured many epidemics over the years. Yellow fever struck during the summer months, but it wasn't until the turn of the twentieth century that scientists understood that yellow fever is caused by mosquito bites. Controlling the mosquito population has helped reduce how often yellow fever strikes.

Whatever the tragic cause, Marie died young, and it seems she was not ready to leave.

Proof? Since the 1960s, four photographs have been taken of a shadowy figure floating out of Room 22 and peeking around a doorway. When you visit Lafitte Guest House, perhaps you will take the fifth photograph of sad, little Marie.

At Houmas House Plantation in Darrow, about an hour west of New Orleans, another little girl, *La Petite Fille*, is seen by tradesmen, staff, and visitors alike. *La Petite Fille* is French for "little girl." When Kevin Kelly purchased the estate, he brought in crews of workers to restore the home. The workers often saw a little girl wander among their tools and materials during construction, and one electrician was so convinced it was a living, breathing girl, he voiced his concerns for her safety.

What a surprise to find out that he was seeing a ghost!

You may see the apparition of *La Petite Fille* come down the spiral staircase inside the house, and if you do, she may ask you to play hide-and-seek with her in the gardens. Some years ago, a medium held a séance in the home. A medium is a person who is believed to be able to communicate with the dead. At the séance, *La Petite Fille* told the medium she would like to play hide-and-seek with Kelly, but he is so big, he scares her a little.

Who is this playful ghost? The owner believes it is May Preston, a little girl who once lived in the home and died of yellow fever at the age of eight.

Proof? The Houmas House historian, Jim Blanchard, acquired an antique doll dress that belonged to the Preston family. And pinned on that dress, he found a handkerchief with the date of May's birthday embroidered on it. At the séance, when the medium held up the dress, the spirit asked, speaking through the medium, "Where is my doll? I've been looking for it for a long time."

May isn't the only ghost at Houmas House Plantation. A spectral riverboat captain has been spotted treading the balcony on the roof, looking toward the Mississippi River that flows nearby. Also, an extremely tall, male Black ghost has been seen often. Blanchard claims to have seen the specter walk through a wall. Later, the historian discovered a secret doorway, right where he saw the phantom disappear. The Black ghost is spotted all around the property, stepping off the front porch and walking through a recently installed courtyard fountain without getting wet.

With Blanchard's help, Kelly has acquired furnishings original to the house; he claims that he's also acquired specters attached to them. One example is a clock that may once have belonged to Napoleon. Blanchard tracked down the clock and carefully packed it for the trip back, removing the pendulum to avoid damaging the clock. After several hours on the road, he arrived at Houmas House Plantation, unpacked the clock, and set it on the dining room mantel. Immediately, the clock began to chime, as if it were glad to be home.

But how? The pendulum was still packed away, separately. The clock should never have been able to chime. The hair began to stand up on the back of Blanchard's neck.

Because not only was the clock chiming, he was also hearing voices... men's voices... a room full of them, talking.

The historian was so spooked he locked the doors, set the house alarm, and headed back to New Orleans as fast as he could.

Wouldn't you?

A House Full of Ghosts

Loyd Hall is a grand plantation about ninety miles northwest of Baton Rouge. The home was built in 1820, but it almost didn't survive its stormy past. The site of elegant dinners and gracious living, the home fell on hard times after the Civil War and was largely forgotten.

In the 1940s, a family purchased the 600 acres that made up the former plantation. They were going to use the land to graze their cattle. To their astonishment, under a thicket of overgrown trees, bushes, vines, and weeds, they found the crumbling Loyd Hall.

The structure was in bad shape but could still be saved—after the family harvested the 200 pounds of honey deposited over the decades by a busy colony of bees! Once renovations began, the owners found intricate woodwork, a grand staircase, ceiling friezes (plaster decorations...

... and a wide assortment of phantoms.

The Loyd Hall ghost lineup begins with William Loyd, who built Loyd Hall. He came to a notorious end here—and seemingly, never left.

William Loyd had mixed loyalties during the Civil War. Sometimes he worked for the Union Army, and sometimes he worked for the Confederate Army. He played one side against the other as he selfishly looked for the best opportunity for himself.

When Loyd Hall became a command post for the Union Army, Loyd saw his chance. The Confederates were camped in the woods nearby, and Loyd decided to see how he could profit from the situation. He snuck between the two armies, acting as a double agent. He found out this was a dangerous game, because the Union Army caught him, tarred and feathered him, and hung him from a tree in the front yard of his own home.

Today, the plantation home is a bed and breakfast. If you want to have a ghostly encounter, book the main bedroom where Loyd's phantom footsteps are often heard pacing back and forth as he awaits his death.

Though Loyd was confined to his bedroom in his final hours, in the afterlife, he is free to roam the building. Witnesses believe he is responsible for the alarming poltergeist activity taking place throughout the home. Poltergeist is a German word that means "noisy ghost." Poltergeists like to break things, move things, and steal things. Residents and visitors to the home are often startled by toppling candlesticks and silverware disappearing from the table; they believe that Loyd is trying to encourage squabbles among friends and family just as he did between the Union and Confederate armies.

Loyd can be such a pest the owners have given him nicknames—"Wily Willie" and "The Doggone Trickster." Curiously, Loyd is sometimes seen as a shaggy, white dog, and sometimes as a shadowy figure, flittering at the corners of witnesses' vision.

So much spirit activity takes place at Loyd Hall, it's hard to understand exactly which restless spirits are responsible. Male apparitions. Female apparitions. Strange white, misty blobs. Soft footsteps, doors opening and closing all by themselves, and cherished objects moving from one place to another.

One ghost that appears at Loyd Hall has been identified as Sally Boston, a Black enslaved woman who served as a nanny. She materializes in a long black dress with a white apron and wears a turban on her head. She died in the home mysteriously—some say she was poisoned. Sally is often seen upstairs in the former nursery, quietly going about the chores involved in looking after children.

Another ghost that has been identified is Anne Loyd. Anne was William Loyd's niece, and she came to a sad end. Jilted by her fiancé, she threw herself from the third-floor window. Today, the third floor is said to be a hub of paranormal activity.

It's one thing to see things or hear things that you can't immediately explain. But as time passes, you might decide that you were mistaken. That your imagination had run wild. But what if you saw, talked with, and became friends with a ghost? And what if you weren't the only one? What would you think if that happened to you?

Well then, meet Harry Henry.

Harry was a young, handsome Union soldier stationed on the Loyd Hall plantation during the Civil War. He often passed the time playing his violin. While awaiting the regiment's next assignment, he fell in love with one of Loyd's nieces. When his regiment pulled out for the next battle, he couldn't bear to leave the girl he loved, and he decided to stay behind. Harry was a deserter. If the army caught him, he would be sentenced to death.

Harry hid in the attic of Loyd Hall. Unfortunately, Grandmother Loyd didn't know the family still had a Union guest. One dark night, they bumped into each other on the stairs. Harry knew it was Grandmother Loyd, but Grandmother Loyd had no idea it was Harry. Battles were taking place all around their home. No one knew from one day to the next who was winning or who was in charge. She thought her home and family were in danger from a mysterious intruder, so she shot him.

Once the lamps were lit and the Loyds saw they had killed a Union soldier; they knew they were in trouble. Would anyone believe Grandmother Loyd had acted in self-defense? The family hurriedly buried Harry in a shallow grave under the house and kept the secret.

Now, at midnight, visitors often hear Harry's footsteps in the attic overhead. He walks to the balcony, where he plays sad music on his violin.

Sometimes, in the family room, Harry partially materializes as a pair of shiny black boots and the tip of a sword.

But Harry isn't always sad—just ask the three ladies who lived in Loyd Hall as children. When they were small, their mother overheard them talking about playing with Harry.

The only problem was, the family did not know anyone named Harry.

The mother asked her daughters—who was this Harry they were talking about? Recounting the story, she says, "They looked at me as if I'd grown two heads and said: 'Mama, Harry is our ghost. He lives on the third floor and plays with us. He's such fun!'"

Later, when they grew up, one of the children added more information. "For years, my sister Paige and I had a playmate who was tall, dark, and dressed in a Union uniform. He was like a big brother to us . . . he was the nicest person."

When you visit Loyd Hall, come in the evening when the sun is going down. As the shadows fall across the home, the spirits of the plantation return. If you're lucky, instead of the spiteful William Loyd, you will meet Harry Henry.

He is the nicest person. Everyone says so.

CHAPTER 6

The Keeper of the Castle

When you visit the Old State Capitol in Baton Rouge, you might find a trail of footprints, spy something flitting in the shadows, or jump when the alarm suddenly blares. But don't worry, it's not an intruder.

It's Pierre, the Keeper of the Castle.

The Old State Capitol sits on a bluff above the Mississippi River. With two towers that look like giant rook chess pieces, black-and-white tiled floors, and a stained-glass dome, the building has acquired the nickname, "The Castle." It was the site of many political fights and wheeling and dealing, and no one was a more talented legislator than Pierre Couvillon.

Pierre had a larger-than-life personality and was a giant of a man who intimidated his opponents with his strong physical presence and intelligence. He served in the Louisiana House of Representatives and Senate from 1834 to 1852, when he suffered a heart attack. Some say he was in the comfort of his own home at the time of his death, but legend has it that Pierre was at the legislature, delivering a passionate speech about fairness for all men. He never finished that speech, so perhaps Pierre's ghost lingers because he feels he has more to say.

Generations of Louisianans have encountered Pierre because he is said to have begun haunting the Old State Capitol soon after his death. Even after the Union Army seized the building and burned it to the ground in 1862, Pierre continued to pace the derelict halls of the capitol, searching for corrupt politicians to scold.

Eventually, The Castle was restored, but the legislature outgrew the space and abandoned it. Years passed, and Pierre was said to still stalk the empty corridors, even though there was no one left to haunt. Then in 1994, The Castle reopened as the Old State Capitol Museum, and right away, employees noticed strange things.

First, a student employee had a weird experience while working in the gift shop. To enter the gift shop, visitors have to pass through a heavy door—a door too heavy to swing on its own. But that's exactly what the gift shop door did—it opened and closed all by itself, often.

One by one, other employees reported strange goings-on to the museum director. Shadows darting through the halls. Disembodied footsteps pounding up and down the spiral staircase. Small items disappearing, only to be found in unusual places.

Whoever is responsible for the unusual happenings, he is particularly fond of stealing tools and hardware, which greatly annoys the maintenance supervisor. Once, the staff of the Old State Capitol Museum hosted a benefit event. The star attraction of the gathering was a valuable painting, which was delivered in a custom-made crate. The maintenance supervisor used a power drill to remove the screws from the top of the crate; he carefully placed the screws on a nearby table. Once the painting was removed from the crate, the maintenance supervisor turned to grab the special screws so he could screw them back into the empty crate for safe keeping.

Half of them were gone.

He and his assistant looked high and low, but they were nowhere to be found. The men shrugged their shoulders, temporarily stowed the painting in the storage room, and went about the building making preparations for the party. Later, when they returned to retrieve the painting so they could set it on display, they had a surprise.

All the missing screws were lined up like toy soldiers on top of the work table.

No one had been in the storage room and the maintenance supervisor was the only one who had the key. As he put it, "I went from a firm believer in not believing to—I'll believe just about anything now."

Over the years, someone unseen has snatched, moved, and rearranged tools, fixtures, and other small items. Who is responsible?

It isn't a big mystery—dozens, maybe hundreds, of people have encountered Pierre over the years. The state archives even issued an official press release in

1996: *Gen. Pierre Couvillon's Ghost Believed to Reside at Old State Capitol.*

Wanda Lee Porter didn't need a press release to know about the Capitol Ghost because she spent a harrowing night chasing him through The Castle.

Wanda was a security guard in the old building. Late one night, she was sitting at the surveillance command center, keeping an eye on the board of lights that signal when a motion detector has been triggered somewhere in The Castle.

Suddenly, one of the lights began to blink—it was surveillance camera number 22. Camera 22 is aimed at the three rooms—two bedrooms and a dining room—that represent the governor's mansion with antique furnishings.

Wanda switched the main monitor to show camera 22's feed so she could see what caused the motion detector to light up. She carefully scanned the video of the bedroom, searching for anyone or anything that could have tripped the alarm. Nothing.

Even though the light on the board continued to blink, Wanda couldn't see the cause. Just as she prepared to go down to the reconstructed rooms to investigate for herself, the light stopped blinking.

Wanda relaxed, but her relief didn't last long. Another alert flashed on the board—this time, it was reporting an intruder in the dining room. Wanda panned the room with her camera, zooming in on the dining room table, and still, she saw nothing.

So, she decided it was time to take a look in person.

First, Wanda made her way to the bedroom. She searched under the bed and behind the curtains. She poked around in each corner. She investigated everywhere someone could hide, but no one was there.

Or so she thought.

Wanda locked the doors and scurried back to her office. By then, the motion detector indicator had stopped blinking. Was she imagining things? Wanda rubbed her chin, wondering what had gotten into her, when—

Blink blink blink.

Startled, Wanda watched as the motion sensor light for camera 21 winked on. She scanned the monitor, but again, no one was there.

Blink!

Another light switched on.

Blink!

And another

Blink!

And another.

One by one, the lights on the security board blinked on and off in progression, as if someone or something were traveling down the hall.

Coming toward Wanda.

As Wanda nervously fingered her flashlight and made plans to confront the intruder, all the lights on the board suddenly blinked off. Which meant whoever—or whatever—was coming her way had stopped at the foot of the staircase.

Wanda waited, but the room was so quiet, the sound of her own nervous breathing filled her ears. Would the trespasser fling the door open to confront her? Would he sneak out of The Castle, unscathed?

Seconds passed, then minutes. Wanda couldn't wait any longer—she had to know what was out there. Carefully, she swung open the security room door and peeked into the hall.

Empty.

She looked over her shoulder at the board and saw that the camera 30 indicator was flashing red—the prowler was in the senate chamber on the second floor.

Wanda knew what she had to do. She was the

only living person in the building and she had to keep it safe. Swiftly and quietly, she made her way down the hall and strode toward the sturdy oak door that shielded the senate chamber. She grabbed the door lever, twisted, and flung herself into the senate room. In one swift motion, Wanda flipped the lights on all at once, hoping to catch the trespasser by surprise.

Instead, she found a small desk behind a wooden guardrail with a portrait of the long-dead senator, Honorable Pierre Couvillon, hanging above it.

And across the polished floor, a trail of footprints that led to the desk.

Spooked, Wanda rushed out of the room, grabbed the telephone, and called the director: "...something is in this building, and I don't know what it is... whatever it is, I'm going to get out of here!"

Before the director could get to The Castle, the

backup security guard appeared. Wanda told him about the blinking lights, the triggered motion detectors, and the eerie trail of footprints. He asked, "What do you think it is?"

Wanda shot back, "What do *you* think it is?"

Neither wanted to be the first to say it, but the facts had become too obvious to deny. Wanda exclaimed, finally, "A ghost, what else?"

Later, Wanda wrote a report on the incident that was sent to the secretary of state of Louisiana. He dispatched an investigator who explored the attic and the rest of the building for hours before finally admitting that something occupies the attic of The Castle.

When you visit The Castle, take the tour to see where it all happened—the governors' rooms, the spiral staircase, and the senate chamber. But stay quiet. Stay alert.

And hold on to your screws.

All Ghosts Are Not the Same

If you're going to live in or visit a haunted house, you have to know what you're dealing with. Some spirits want to terrify you. They rattle their chains, bang on walls, and might even try to knock you down. Some spirits simply want you to leave them alone to rest in peace, and when you don't, they get cranky. Some spirits want to help you. They find lost things. They keep you from harm. And sometimes, they give you great advice.

Ormond Plantation is near Destrehan, about twenty-three miles west of New Orleans. This place has a tragic past, and perhaps that's why a terrifying ghost haunts the grounds. Pierre Trepagnier built the home in 1790. An important person, he hosted equally important guests and extravagant parties. However, one night, a servant notified Trepagnier that a Spanish carriage and horses had appeared at the door. Trepagnier went to investigate and never returned. He disappeared without a trace.

When the next owner took possession of Ormond Plantation, a yellow fever epidemic tore through the area. The owner decided to pack up his family and leave; however, the sickness followed him and he died of yellow fever soon after.

The property passed through several hands until it was finally bought in 1898 by Basile

LaPlace Jr., a Louisiana state senator. Within a year of buying the plantation, LaPlace was dead, shot and hung from an oak tree on the Great Mississippi River Road. Some say he was killed by a political enemy, and others say LaPlace was having an affair with the caretaker's daughter and her angry father took his revenge.

As you may expect, many believe the restless spirits of these former owners still remain. Once, a séance was held in the home. The dining room table was cleared to make room for the medium's tools: flickering candles and a smoldering incense dish warding off evil spirits.

The evening began with a retelling of the strange disappearance of Trepagnier. When the storyteller got to the part where Trepagnier walked out the Ormond Plantation door for the last time, the incense dish exploded with a loud *pop*! As if to let the attendees know that Trepagnier had returned to his home after all.

Another spooky incident happened on the verandah. A docent named Edith Layton was leading a tour of the plantation, explaining its history and the many precious antiques the building houses. But one visitor was much more interested to know about the resident phantoms.

As Layton good-humoredly told the group about some frightening experiences she'd had, she heard a thunderous noise—but no one else on the verandah seemed to hear it. As the tour group chatted among themselves, and Layton turned to look down the porch, the nerve-shattering noise roared toward them. Suddenly, Layton's knees buckled as she felt something strange and powerful rush right through her.

Was it one of the former masters of the plantation, angry that she was spilling all their haunting secrets?

At Madewood, a grand manor house in Napoleonville, about seventy-miles west of New

Orleans, you'll find a ghost that simply wants to be left alone: Colonel Thomas Pugh, the former owner. Like so many stately homes in the area, Madewood had fallen into disrepair. Many potential buyers wanted to dismantle the home and sell the materials for profit. But one woman decided to restore Madewood to its former glory.

Part of that restoration involved clearing away decades of weeds, leaves, and the rotting logs of long-fallen trees from the family graveyard. The Pughs had slept in silent repose in the family plot since the 1840s, unbothered. No one even remembered that the cemetery existed. The new owner cleared the debris from the family tombs out of respect, but it seems Colonel Pugh was not happy.

The owner and some of her guests felt Colonel Pugh's displeasure one evening at dinner. The table was spread with sparkling china and silver piled high with scrumptious food, and in the center sat a fantastic cranberry-colored glass epergne (pronounced eh-PERN), which is a fancy centerpiece that might hold fruit, flowers, candles, or desserts.

The group ate and talked, having a lovely time, until gradually, one by one, they fell silent as they noticed the epergne slowly lift into the air, all on its own. It hovered for a moment, and then gently, carefully, sank to the floor, unharmed.

Apparently, Colonel Pugh had a message to get across. He wanted his family to rest unseen and unknown, and he didn't appreciate the attention they now received from Madewood residents and visitors.

If you're looking for a helpful ghost, check out Lanaux Mansion in the French Quarter in New Orleans. Ruth, the owner, depends on her otherworldly resident for decorating tips.

Lanaux Mansion was once owned by Charles A. Johnson, a demanding man who took pride in his home. A century later, when Ruth fell in love with the home and bought it, she didn't know that she was also acquiring an invisible partner.

Johnson was known to have exquisite taste, and he left behind a library of books on interior decorating published in the 1870s, when Lanaux Mansion was built. In these books, Johnson earmarked pages and left notations about how the home should be outfitted—suggestions for drapes, carpeting, and furniture. Ruth uses these reference books to guide her in decorating decisions so she will end up with a home that pleases her—and Johnson.

When Ruth wants to start on a big project, she sits quietly in the gold-draped parlor next to the nine-foot grand piano and listens. Johnson always comes through with the best solutions for renovating Lanaux Mansion.

For instance, Ruth had decided she needed a dining room rug that would fit the color scheme and theme of the room. She asked Johnson, "You know the finances and the funds. Do you think we can find a twenty-one-by-fourteen-foot rug for the dining room at a fair price?" Within days, she found herself at a store with the exact rug she needed, at the exact price she wanted to pay.

Johnson has only materialized once, but it was memorable. One Saturday morning, Ruth was busy working upstairs. She realized that she needed something from the first floor, so she started down the staircase. At the landing, something caught her eye.

Something slowly traveling up the stairs to the third-floor attic.

It was a faint mist, but in that mist, she saw a man wearing a short, English walking coat cropped above the knee. She wasn't frightened, but she was curious. Who could this eerie presence be?

Three months later, the descendant of a

former owner called Ruth and offered her a portrait of Charles A. Johnson that had once hung in the parlor of Lanaux Mansion.

She leaped at the chance. Finally, she would see the face of the man who had been communicating with her all this time, whose taste she admired, and who had expertly advised her on how to restore the lovely home. Guess what she saw when she looked at the painting? The portrait of the man she had seen on the stairs, down to the English walking coat.

Three different hauntings, three different experiences. Whenever you visit a haunted location, stay on your toes. Depending on the ghosts, you might be scolded, or you might be scared out of your wits. But if you're lucky, you will get the best advice of your life.

From the dead.

Love Gone Wrong

Visit New Orleans Creole Cookery, a restaurant on Toulouse Street in New Orleans, and you will enjoy fine dining. A relaxed atmosphere. Soul-stirring music. And perhaps, the supernatural echoes of a love triangle that ended in tragedy.

Who is responsible for the strange happenings on Toulouse Street? We know that the building was erected in the 1700s, and Mary, a widow married three times, inherited it from her second husband after his death in 1806. We know that she married Joseph soon after. And we know that Joseph was seeing another woman, Angelique.

Things did not work out well.

Mary was a beautiful, proud, independent woman who owned her own property, which was somewhat unusual. She did not know that Joseph was involved with another woman, because if she had, she would not have tolerated it.

The other woman, Angelique, was a mixed-race beauty. At the time, people's social status was very much tied to their race. Angelique did not have many options, so she chose to live her life as Joseph's "other wife." Angelique's job was to provide a place to get away for Joseph and be available whenever he wanted to stay with her. Joseph's job was to provide Angelique with money and protection. The arrangement went smoothly for a while, but then a complication arose.

Angelique fell in love with Joseph.

Angelique began to dream about becoming Joseph's wife. Now, she was a secret hidden in the shadows. If she were Joseph's legal wife, she would be respected in the community and could walk down the street with her head held high.

Unfortunately, Joseph thought their alliance was purely a business relationship. He provided a house, food, and necessities, and Angelique provided companionship. But Angelique had developed real feelings for Joseph, and she wanted their relationship to be more than a business transaction. She wanted Joseph to divorce Mary and marry her.

Joseph refused.

Angelique was furious and went to his home to confront him. She argued. She cried.

She pleaded. She screamed. Finally, she gave Joseph an ultimatum—either confess everything to Mary, divorce her, and marry Angelique, or Angelique would tell Mary about their arrangement.

Joseph was incensed. Mary would never forgive Joseph for cheating on her. It would be the end of his marriage to the vital, fascinating woman.

He snapped. In a rage, Joseph rushed toward Angelique, clamped his strong hands around her slender neck, and squeezed.

When Angelique had taken her last breath, Joseph crept into the courtyard under cover of the moonless night and buried her in the garden along the rear wall. However, a teenager walking by saw him. Suspicious of a man who was digging a hole in the middle of the night, the boy ran off to tell the authorities.

Joseph panicked—there was a witness! He

would never be able to talk his way out of this predicament. He would be arrested and tried for murder. Mary would find out how he had betrayed her and would divorce him.

Mary would be gone. Angelique would be gone. His life would be in ruins.

All of Joseph's sins and betrayals came crashing down on him, and it was too much to bear. He climbed to the third floor, draped a noose around his neck, and jumped.

Even though this tragic story happened two hundred years ago, Mary, Joseph, and Angelique still haunt the building on Toulouse Street. We know this because owners, workers, and visitors have reported unsettling incidents over the years.

Visit the restaurant to see for yourself. There's a good chance you will have a spooky experience. Here are a few tips to help you identify which unfortunate spirit you have met.

You'll recognize Joseph because he is the grouchy one. Perhaps he's still annoyed that his arrangement with Angelique fell apart, or perhaps he always was a bit of a jerk. He tends to stay on the third floor, which is a storage room. You should probably skip touring this part of the building, because employees report feeling an evil force there. They avoid climbing to the third floor as much as they can, leaving Joseph to stew in his shame for murdering a woman who loved him.

Maybe you'll run into Mary, who was innocent in this whole affair and seems to be stuck reexperiencing the heartbreaking drama that occurred so long ago. Still jealous after all these centuries, she is known to throw books at customers in the gift shop. But she doesn't throw books at just anybody; her targets are always attractive ladies who remind her of the beautiful woman who cast a fateful spell over her husband.

If you're lucky, you might cross paths with a full-bodied apparition of Angelique, the woman whose unrequited love set the grisly murder-suicide in motion. Angelique loves music, especially soulful, sad ballads. She is often spotted hanging over the banister, watching musicians play in the courtyard below—where it is said her bones still lie. Some report hearing her wistful sighs as she listens to the heart-wrenching lyrics of a love ballad. Finally, when she has had enough, she disappears, once again an eternal victim of unrequited love.

Restless in the City of the Dead

If you find yourself in Metairie Cemetery after dark, you should be worried. The narrow lanes that meander through this City of the Dead are peaceful and welcoming in the light of day but eerie at night. Once the tourists have left, the resident specters roam the grounds, and they might not be pleased to see you. Especially one ghost, who is still searching for a peaceful final resting place.

New Orleans is an exciting place with a rough-and-tumble past. And the fascinating characters who built the city over the centuries were tough, hard-working people who made New Orleans the unique and exciting city that it is today. Josie Arlington is one of those fascinating characters.

We know she was born Mamie Duebler at the end of the Civil War. Raised in a conservative family, her life took a turn when she left home at seventeen. One account states that she fell in love with a scoundrel named Philip Lobrano

and ran away to live with him. But another story insists that Mamie had simply been out for the evening and arrived home after curfew. Her strict father decided to punish her for breaking the rules. No matter how loudly she beat on the door to come inside, he ignored her. She was never allowed in his home again.

Whether she ran away for love or suffered the wrath of her father, Mamie was on her own.

She quickly changed her name to Josie Alton and went to work in sinister, grimy places in the French Quarter. The French Quarter is the oldest neighborhood in New Orleans and is still where *les bons moments roulent* (that means "good times roll" in French).

Josie quickly gained a reputation—she was a stunning young woman with a very fiery temper. She was fiercely competitive with women she worked with, and arguments often came to blows. In one notable street brawl, most of Josie's hair was pulled out, and the other woman ended up with parts of an ear and her lower lip missing.

Life was tough in the French Quarter of New Orleans.

In the following years, Josie opened a series of businesses under the names Josie Lobrano, Josi Lobrano d'Arlington, and then finally, Josie Arlington. Each business was a little higher class than the last one. She prospered and bought a home in a respectable neighborhood, but to her irritation, she was not accepted into decent society.

In 1905, a fire ripped through Josie's business, and she barely escaped with her life. It was the first time Josie had ever come close to death, and the experience rattled her. Josie became obsessed with dying, the afterlife, and where she would have her final resting place.

New Orleans is famous for its Cities of the Dead, which are dozens of cemeteries that guard the remains of those who came before. Here, people are laid to rest in aboveground tombs that often look like miniature mansions, with doors, pillars, and imitation windows. The City of New Orleans lies below sea level, and underground water is very near the surface. If you try to dig a grave, it will quickly fill with water. Coffins buried belowground will not stay buried. They will soon rise, pushed by the water beneath them, and resurface into the open air.

The mausoleums built in the Cities of the Dead usually house the remains of many generations of the same family. How do they fit so many people in these tombs? They follow the year-and-a-day rule. By custom, one year after burial, a body may be removed. The casket is opened and the bones that remain are put into another container, usually a plastic pouch. This pouch is then laid on a shelf built in the back of the tomb, and the casket is destroyed.

After the life-changing fire, Josie bought a $2,000 plot—that would be more than $60,000 today—in Metairie Cemetery on Pontchartrain Boulevard. Josie spent a fortune hiring a German designer and Italian artist to help her design her

tomb and paid for an army of workmen to finish it quickly.

When you visit, Josie's tomb will be easy to spot. Four steps lead up to the heavy, bronze doors that secure the crypt. The mausoleum is carved from reddish-brown marble brought to New Orleans all the way from Maine. Marble pillars frame the doors, and atop the pillars sit identical urns with carved replicas of fire. Just outside the doors of the mausoleum, carrying a basket of flowers and reaching timidly toward the doors but not quite touching them, is a life-sized bronze statue of a woman. Many believe the woman represents Josie as she enters the afterlife.

Three years after the tomb was finished, Josie died on February 14, 1914—Valentine's Day. The haunting began soon after.

Josie's body was barely cold in her coffin when witnesses reported that the stone flames atop her tomb were glowing red. The news spread, and night after night, more and more gawkers gathered to witness the disturbing phenomenon themselves.

The people who took care of Metairie Cemetery were annoyed. They did not appreciate the morbid attention Josie Arlington was bringing to their dignified cemetery. Finally, a cemetery official decided that the cause of the glowing flames was actually a new toll barrier that had been installed on a nearby road. The red signal beacon on the barrier was reflecting off the polished granite mausoleum.

But if that were the answer, why didn't the light reflect on the other family crypts in the area? Why did it only light up the flames on Josie's tomb?

The red signal beacon on the toll barrier was removed, and cemetery officials carved a cross on the back of Josie's tomb as a gris-gris (pronounced GREE-gree) to appease the onlookers. A gris-gris is a Voodoo amulet that repels evil. This step made the public happy, and the morbid spectators disappeared. It seemed that Josie would finally rest in peace, but fate had other plans.

Josie left her fortune to her niece, who promptly squandered it. When the niece ran out of cash, she sold Josie's beautiful home. Once the money from the sale of the home was gone, the only thing the niece had left was Josie's tomb at Metairie Cemetery, which she sold to a wealthy family.

What a betrayal! In the final years of Josie's life, all she'd thought about was building a suitable place where she could rest through eternity. But a year and a day after her burial, someone else owned her cherished tomb! They etched their name over the doors, removed

Josie's body, packed her remains in a small bag, and destroyed her coffin.

Now the problem was, where would Josie's remains go? The new owners didn't want them. And the cemetery had been attracting way too much-unwanted attention over Josie. So, cemetery officials buried her remains in a place that remains secret to this day.

But that is not the end of the story. Josie is not one to quietly recede into the pages of history. She worked hard all her life, fighting for every penny she ever made and enduring hardship and heartbreak. And she is still fighting to fulfill her final wishes.

Cemetery workers and visitors report that they have seen the statue outside Josie's tomb come to life and take a stroll around the grounds. Is she searching for her missing remains? Is she determined to find a door that will open when she knocks?

If you find yourself in Metairie Cemetery one night, stay alert. Shadows and shapes lurk among the crypts. If you listen, you may hear soft sobbing in the wind. And if you run into a woman in a flowing robe carrying a basket of flowers as she wanders the deserted streets, be respectful. It is Josie, still looking for a place to rest.

A Ghostly Goodbye

Millions of tourists flock to Louisiana every year to enjoy delicious food, lively music, inspiring art, and intriguing history. But some visitors—like you—know Louisiana offers so much more.

If you know where to look, you'll find haunts, ghosts, and *les rougarou*. But are they real? Would a photograph with a faint, mysterious lady looking out a window persuade you? Or the testimony of a witness, still spooked by the sad strains of music played on a phantom violin? What would it take to convince you? In the end, each of us has to weigh the facts and decide—are ghosts and other strange beings real?

What do you believe?

Lisha Cauthen has explored Louisiana's haunted plantations, shuddered through New Orleans's spooky cemeteries, and investigated the ghost-filled streets of the French Quarter. She currently writes in the attic of a 100-year-old house built on a Civil War battlefield in Kansas City, Missouri. Which is only a little bit haunted. This is her fifth book of Ghostly Tales in the *Spooky America* series.

Check out some of the other *Spooky America* titles available now!

Spooky America was adapted from the creeptastic *Haunted America* series for adults. *Haunted America* explores historical haunts in cities and regions across America. Here's more from the original *Haunted Louisiana* author, Barbara Sillery:

  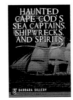  

www.barbarasillery.com